DK SUPERGUIDES
INLINE SKATING

Stroking and gliding

*Removing the
back brake*

*Learning
to jump*

*Regaining
your balance*

Parallel turn

Heel stop

*Announcing
your intentions*

*Stepping
over a twig*

DK SUPERGUIDES
INLINE SKATING

Written by Dawn Irwin
Foreword by Chris Edwards

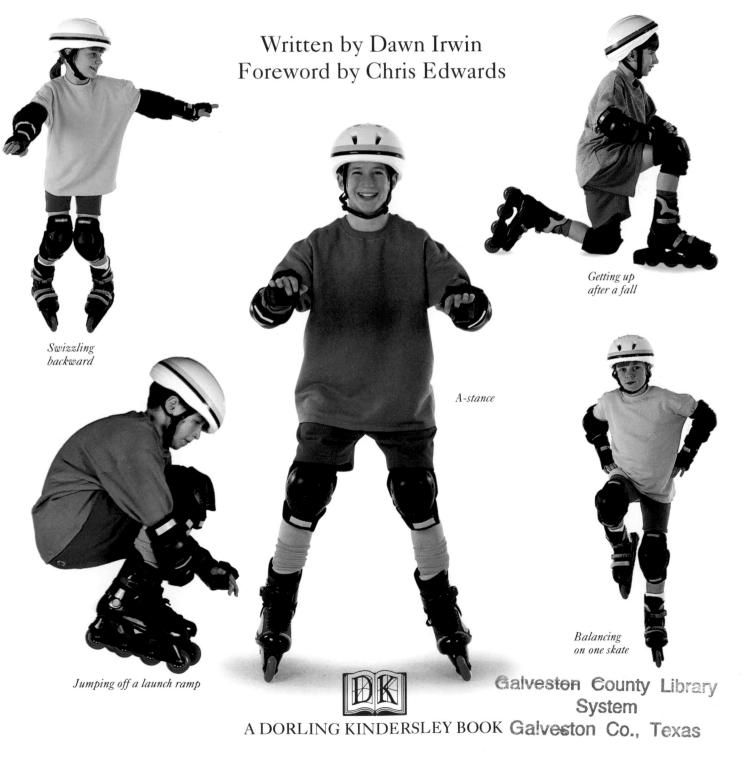

Swizzling backward

Getting up after a fall

A-stance

Jumping off a launch ramp

Balancing on one skate

DK

A DORLING KINDERSLEY BOOK

Dorling DK Kindersley

LONDON, NEW YORK, SYDNEY, DELHI, PARIS,
MUNICH and JOHANNESBURG

Project Editor Fiona Robertson, Lee Simmons
Art Editors Cheryl Telfer, Rebecca Johns
Photography Ray Moller
Picture Research Helen Stallion
Production Charlotte Traill, Orla Creegan
US Editor Camela Decaire

The young inline skaters
James Hall, Simeon Hartwig, Barry Lee Normah, Peter Royal, and Kelly Wiles

Dorling Kindersley would like to thank Bauer for supplying
all the skates and protective gear used in this book.

Published in the United States by
Dorling Kindersley Publishing, Inc
95 Madison Avenue, New York, New York 10016

First published as *The Young Inline Skater*, 1996
First American Edition, 1996
Revised American Edition, 2000
2 4 6 8 10 9 7 5 3 1

Dorling Kindersley books are available at special discounts for bulk purchases for sales promotions or
premiums. Special editions, including personalized covers, excerpts of existing guides, and corporate
imprints can be created in large quantities for specific needs. For more information, contact Special Markets
Dept./Dorling Kindersley Publishing, Inc./95 Madison Ave,/New York, NY 10016/Fax: 800-600-9098.

ISBN 0-7894-6542-6

Color reproduction by Colourscan, Singapore
Printed and bound in Italy by L.E.G.O.

see our complete
catalog at
www.dk.com

Contents

To all young inline skaters

"THERE IS NOTHING more exhilarating than catching some big air over a half pipe ramp. Yet there is a lot more to inline skating than wild stunts. Inline skating is about physical fitness, good sportsmanship, discipline, and hard work. As with any sport, you have got to have the right equipment, the patience to learn the basic skills, and the time to practice as much as you can, so that you can be at your best in performance, competition, or in the park. It doesn't matter where you skate, it's how you skate. If you put in the effort, the rewards of this sport can be terrific. The videos, films, and Team Rollerblade® activities that I have been able to participate in have more than compensated for all the hours of hard work. I hope this book will inspire you and get you rolling!"

"I started skating when I was 13 years old. I knew right away inline skating was going to become a favorite pastime –even a career!"

"Some tricks, such as the Mute Grab that I'm doing here, are performed off a platform called a launch box."

"This trick is called a Japan Air. It takes a lot of momentum to propel yourself up this high. You need to build up terrific speed on the take-off to get this move off the ground."

"The Frontside Grind is another fun stunt, but remember you should never try any of these tricks without proper safety equipment and instruction. They might look effortless here, but they require lots of practice!"

"The Sad Plant Invert is one of my favorite tricks. It has it all – speed, height, power, and grace. Hang onto your helmets, because you're in for quite a ride with this freewheeling maneuver!"

History of inline skating

THE FIRST ROLLER, or "quad," skate was developed in the 1700s by a Belgian named Joseph Merlin. Merlin was a great ice-skater and he wanted to find a way to skate during the warm summer months. His idea, to attach wooden spools to his shoes, seemed ingenious, but he could not turn or stop, so he fell many times! The first inline skate was developed in France in 1819, followed in 1823 by a five-wheeled invention by Englishman Robert John Tyers. However, turning and stopping were still a problem, and because the skates were made of iron, they were extremely unstable. The modern inline skate was developed in the 1980s by two American hockey players, Scott and Brennan Olson. Unlike the early models, today's skates are fast, smooth, and lightweight.

A fashionable hobby
Ice-skating was used as a means of travel in Scandinavia as far back as 1100 BC, but it was not until the early 19th century that it became a popular and fashionable pastime.

The iron wheels had no bearings and were probably noisy as well as difficult to get rolling.

Early inline skate
Early inline skates had just two iron wheels and a leather strap to go around the ankle and lower leg. Because there was no heel brake, turning and stopping were very difficult!

A competitive edge
Roller-skating became much easier after the invention of wheel bearings in 1884. By 1947, roller-skating featured in competitions, such as this women's race in the US.

A perfect fit?
Imagine how uncomfortable this skate from 1879 must have been. It is made from a high-heeled shoe with wheels fitted underneath and a strap around the ankle.

The front stopper shown here has now been replaced by a back heel brake.

Early roller-skating rink
The roller rink shown here was built at Crystal Palace, in London, in 1890. The floor was wooden and the rink was long and narrow, much like skating rinks today. Skaters wore iron quad skates, with two wheels on either side of the skate boot.

Modern inline skate
Scott and Brennan Olson, two devoted ice hockey players from Minneapolis, Minnesota, developed the first modern inline skates, which they called "Rollerblades®". Their design was based on that of an ice hockey skate.

Starting out

INLINE SKATING is one of the most exciting, fastest-growing sports today. It's also fun and easy to learn. The most important piece of equipment is your skates, which must fit properly and be comfortable. You should also have the correct safety gear to protect you from injury. Combine these with layers of loose, comfortable clothes that allow plenty of movement, and you're ready to start out.

Most helmets have foam pads and adjustable straps to guarantee a good fit.

A long-sleeved top will protect your skin if you fall.

Helmet
The helmet is the most important part of your safety gear. It must comply with safety standards, and fit your head securely and comfortably.

Elbow pads
Elbow pads offer valuable protection for your sensitive elbow joints. Like knee pads, they should be worn with the holes pointing downward.

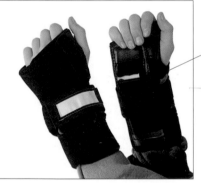

The plastic bump on the wrist guard should be under your palm.

Wrist guards
Hands and wrists are the areas most likely to get injured in a fall. Wrist guards have strong plastic pieces on the underside to protect you.

A money belt is useful for carrying any small items such as keys or change.

Before you buy them, make sure that your skates fit properly and are supportive, particularly around the ankle.

Baggy shorts are ideal in warm weather and do not restrict movement.

A tight fit
Both elbow and knee pads have strong elastic to help secure them to your arm or leg and are fastened with Velcro®. Make sure they are not too tight, or they could restrict your movements when skating.

Knee pads
Try to wear knee pads that have a fabric cushion covered by a hard plastic cup. The cushion absorbs the impact of a fall, and the plastic protects your skin and clothes.

A frame at the bottom of the skate holds the wheels in place. Most frames are about 12 in (30 cm) long.

Night gear

When skating at night, you must be sure that you can be clearly seen by drivers, cyclists, and pedestrians. It is often colder at night, so you should dress appropriately.

Wear a scarf or turtleneck to keep your neck warm.

A warm, light-colored jacket is ideal for skating at night.

A reflective strap or vest is very important when skating at night – it allows people in front of you and behind you to see you.

If you are wearing gloves, put them on under your wrist guards.

Sweatpants or leggings are ideal for chilly evenings.

Be careful not to tighten the ankle strap too much, or you will not be able to skate correctly.

Tighten the middle strap the most so that your foot feels secure.

Heel brake

Inline skates

Most inline skates have a hard outer shell and a soft inner liner for support and comfort. The skates can be tightened with laces or buckles, or both. The right skate usually has a heel brake.

Leave the toe strap loose to avoid cramping.

Different types of wheels

Wheels

Your wheels have the greatest effect on your performance. Wheel sizes are measured in millimeters. The bigger the wheel, the faster it will go. Wheels also come in varying degrees of durometer, or hardness, ranging from 74A to 93A. The lower the durometer, the softer the wheel.

Reflective strips can be attached to your wrist pads.

Be seen
A good bike shop should stock all the lights and reflective strips that you need.

Knee pads often have reflective strips sown onto the Velcro® straps.

Skate light

Helmet light

It is extremely important to be visible from behind when you skate at night. Attach a light to an elastic strap around your helmet.

Skate light

Use a reflective Velcro® strap to attach a light to your skate. This will help to prevent it from bouncing off when you hit a bump.

Safe skating

SKATERS SHOULD FOLLOW a simple set of rules that will allow them to enjoy the sport safely and without injury to themselves or others. This not only sets a good example, it encourages others to try inline skating by demonstrating that it is a safe, fun activity. In addition, skaters who wear protective gear are much less likely to become injured. Protected skaters enjoy skating more because they are more relaxed and can skate with greater confidence.

Top ten tips
1. Always wear protective gear: helmet, knee and elbow pads, and wrist guards.
2. Learn the basic skills in a safe, flat area.
3. Keep your skates and equipment in proper working order.
4. Stay away from traffic.
5. Watch out for hazards like water, oil, and sand.
6. Don't skate if it's wet.
7. Always skate in control.
8. Stay alert and be courteous at all times.
9. Cross roads at suitable crossings.
10. Always yield or stop to allow pedestrians to pass.

Indicate your intentions clearly so that other skaters are not taken by surprise.

Announce your intentions
Always pass pedestrians, cyclists, and other skaters on the left. Announce your intentions by saying, for example, "Passing on your left". Pass only when it is safe and you have enough room to do so.

Master the basics
It is essential to learn the basic skating skills in a large, flat area that is free of obstacles and away from traffic. You will feel much safer and have plenty of room to move around. As your skills improve, so will your confidence and you can progress to more advanced terrain.

Basic inline equipment
It is a good idea to put together a skate repair kit, which you can carry in your skate bag. Make sure you buy the correct tools for your skates. Some general tools are shown below. Check with your local skate store for more specialized tools.

Tool bag

Three-way tool   *Bearings*   *Container for spare bearings*

A selection of different Allen keys

Carrying your gear
In addition to your tools, you may want to carry other items, such as some money and a drink. You could use a personal stereo bag for this purpose, and a skate bag for your skates.

Tool bag to fit around boot

Skate bag

Skate care

Skates actually require very little maintenance. Any repairs that you do need to carry out will probably be fairly inexpensive. Keep your skates clean by wiping them occasionally with a soft, damp cloth. The most important area to check is the wheels. Look at them once a week for wear on the inside edges. Spin each wheel to make sure it is moving freely and listen for any grinding or gritty sounds that suggest the bearings are dirty.

Hold your skates at eye level to check them.

Changing wheels

1 Whether you are rotating an existing set of wheels or replacing them with a completely new set, it is useful to know how to change your wheels. Hold the skate firmly between your legs and use the appropriate Allen wrench to unscrew the wheel bolt.

Insert the Allen wrench into the bolt to unscrew it.

2 Work on one wheel at a time. When you have unscrewed the bolt, remove it and lift out the wheel. To replace the wheel, insert it back into the frame and tighten each bolt as far as you can. When all the wheels are back in place, adjust each bolt slightly so that each wheel spins for the same length of time.

Lift the whole wheel out.

Wheel rotation

Rotating your wheels means changing their position on the skate frame and turning them over so that their edges wear evenly. Inside wheel edges wear out more quickly than those on the outside edges, so rotating them makes them last longer.

The arrows show the positions to which the wheels move after they have been rotated.

④ ③ ② ①

Wheel rotation chart

Number the wheel positions from front to back, so that the toe wheel is number one, as shown above. Following the chart shown right, move wheel number one to position number three on the other skate; wheel number two becomes number four, and so on until all the wheels have been rotated.

Old position on skate	New position on other skate
1 →	3
2 →	4
3 →	1
4 →	2

Cleaning and replacing bearings

Each skate wheel has two sets of tiny round metal bearings. These enable the wheel to spin smoothly. The condition of your bearings has a tremendous effect on the speed at which you skate. Dirt in your bearings not only slows you down, it will also eventually destroy the bearings. Most bearings are sealed inside a casing designed to repel dirt, but if you do skate through dust, sand, or water, it's best to clean them right away.

1 The outer bearings casing tends to attract a lot of dust. You should wipe it down regularly with a dry cloth or a clean paper towel. A toothbrush is also useful for cleaning inside the grooves.

2 To clean or change all the bearings, use a three-way tool (see page 14) to pop the bearings out on both sides. Clean the bearings with a dry cloth, but don't oil them. When you replace them, be careful not to tighten the bolt too much.

Removing the back brake

Back brakes can be either square or round. When your brake has worn below the halfway mark, you should either replace it (if it is the square brake), or turn it around to expose more rubber (if it is the round brake).

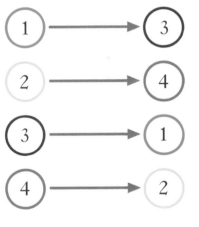

Remove the back brake in the same way as the wheels. Make sure you use the correct Allen wrench.

Hold the skate firmly between your legs.

Warming up

INLINE SKATING is a very physical activity that uses lots of muscles in your body. Before you put your skates on, it is therefore important to spend time stretching and warming up. This will keep you from injuring yourself and also make you feel more relaxed and confident when you skate. The stretches shown here will loosen the major muscles used while skating.

Hamstring stretch

To stretch the large hamstring muscle at the back of your thigh, lie on your back with one knee bent. Raise the other leg in the air. Hold the leg behind your knee and gently pull it back.

Try to keep this leg only slightly bent to make sure you stretch the muscle.

Be sure to keep this foot on the floor.

Keep your back straight.

Hamstring and calf stretch

Placing your hands on your left thigh for support, bend your left leg and extend your right leg out in front of you. Push your hips backward until you feel a stretch in the hamstring at the back of your right thigh. If you lift your toe, you will also feel a stretch in your calf, or lower leg, muscle.

This leg should be bent for support.

Lift up your toe to increase the stretch.

Side bends

With your feet apart and your knees bent, reach one arm into the air and stretch over to the other side. Remember to stretch up from your waist. Keep your hips steady and facing forward. Hold the stretch for 20 seconds, then repeat on the other side.

Try not to lean forward as you stretch up.

Double-sided
All of these stretches should be repeated on your other side.

Place this hand on your hip.

Bend your knees slightly.

Arm circling

Your arms should be close to your ears.

Don't forget to swing your arms forward, too.

Try to breathe normally throughout this exercise.

1 Stand up straight with your knees slightly bent. Raise your arms straight out in front of you.

2 Keep your arms straight and bring them above your head as you start to circle them backward.

3 Finish the circle by bringing your arms backward and down to the sides. Repeat 10 times.

 **Time scale**
Hold each stretch for about 15-20 seconds.

16

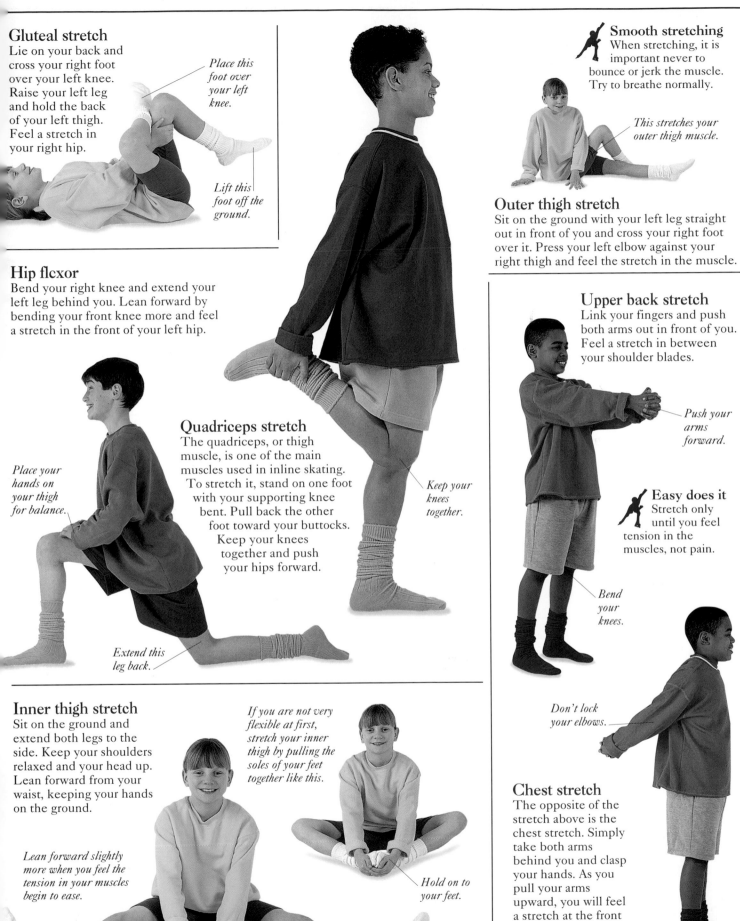

Gluteal stretch
Lie on your back and cross your right foot over your left knee. Raise your left leg and hold the back of your left thigh. Feel a stretch in your right hip.

Place this foot over your left knee.

Lift this foot off the ground.

Hip flexor
Bend your right knee and extend your left leg behind you. Lean forward by bending your front knee more and feel a stretch in the front of your left hip.

Place your hands on your thigh for balance.

Quadriceps stretch
The quadriceps, or thigh muscle, is one of the main muscles used in inline skating. To stretch it, stand on one foot with your supporting knee bent. Pull back the other foot toward your buttocks. Keep your knees together and push your hips forward.

Keep your knees together.

Extend this leg back.

Smooth stretching
When stretching, it is important never to bounce or jerk the muscle. Try to breathe normally.

This stretches your outer thigh muscle.

Outer thigh stretch
Sit on the ground with your left leg straight out in front of you and cross your right foot over it. Press your left elbow against your right thigh and feel the stretch in the muscle.

Upper back stretch
Link your fingers and push both arms out in front of you. Feel a stretch in between your shoulder blades.

Push your arms forward.

Easy does it
Stretch only until you feel tension in the muscles, not pain.

Bend your knees.

Don't lock your elbows.

Chest stretch
The opposite of the stretch above is the chest stretch. Simply take both arms behind you and clasp your hands. As you pull your arms upward, you will feel a stretch at the front of your shoulders and across your chest.

Inner thigh stretch
Sit on the ground and extend both legs to the side. Keep your shoulders relaxed and your head up. Lean forward from your waist, keeping your hands on the ground.

Lean forward slightly more when you feel the tension in your muscles begin to ease.

If you are not very flexible at first, stretch your inner thigh by pulling the soles of your feet together like this.

Hold on to your feet.

Ready to roll

NOW THAT YOU HAVE your skates and protective gear on, it's time to learn the basics. The first thing you need to learn is how to stand correctly. This will help you keep your balance, which in turn will improve your confidence. Practice at first on a patch of grass so that your skates do not roll out of control. Try to stay relaxed, and always remember to keep your head up and your eyes focused on the way ahead – not on your skates!

Edges

Look straight down your wheels. You will see that the middle of the wheel is narrow and the sides are sloping. These are your wheel edges.

Your feet should be shoulder-width apart.

Push your ankles outward.

Center edges
The narrow part of the wheel is the center edge. Try to stand on the highest part of your skates, and you will be on your center edges.

Outside edges
With your feet together, push your ankles outward. You are on your outside edges. With experience, you will use your outside edges more.

The ready position

Every move in inline skating starts and finishes with the ready position. In this position, your upper body, legs, and arms should be balanced and centered over your skates. This helps you control your skates, whatever the speed and conditions.

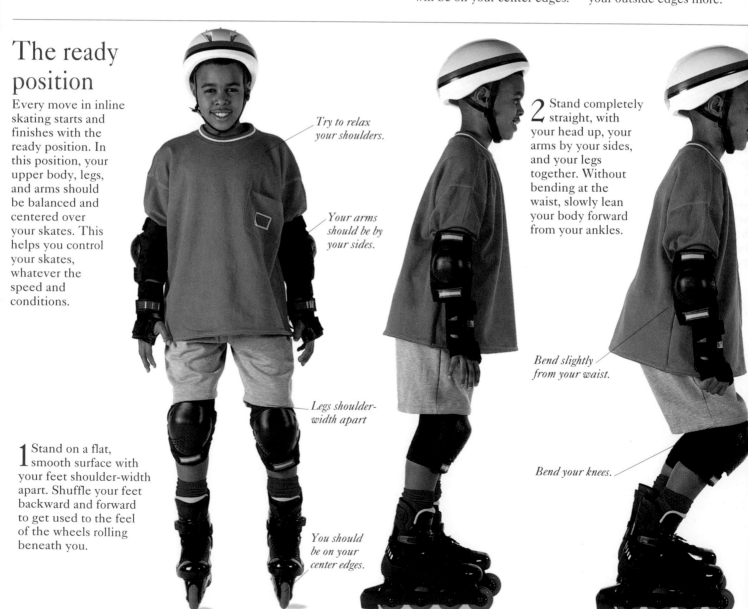

Try to relax your shoulders.

Your arms should be by your sides.

Legs shoulder-width apart

1 Stand on a flat, smooth surface with your feet shoulder-width apart. Shuffle your feet backward and forward to get used to the feel of the wheels rolling beneath you.

You should be on your center edges.

2 Stand completely straight, with your head up, your arms by your sides, and your legs together. Without bending at the waist, slowly lean your body forward from your ankles.

Bend slightly from your waist.

Bend your knees.

Practice finding your corresponding edges on the other side, too.

Roll your ankles inward slightly.

Inside edges

Stand with your feet wider than your shoulders, and roll your ankles inward so that you are on your inside edges. You will be on these edges about 60% of the time.

Corresponding edges

With your feet about 6 in (15 cm) apart, push your left ankle inward and your right ankle outward. These are your corresponding edges, which you use when you turn.

Stances

When you are confident in the ready position, try these different feet positions, or stances. Remember to keep your knees bent, your head up, and your arms out in front of you.

V-stance

When you take your first skating step, you will start from the V-stance. Stand with your feet together and your toes turned outward. Roll your wheels onto their inside edges.

Inside edges

A-stance

When you first learn to turn, you will use the A-stance, in which your feet are wider than your shoulders, to help you feel more stable. You should be on your inside edges.

Inside edges

Nose to toes
In this position, try to keep your nose, knees, and toes in a straight line.

3 Now bend your knees and repeat the movement until you can feel your shins pressing against the tongues of your skates. If you look down, you should only be able to see the tops of your knee pads. Try to bend slightly from your waist, too.

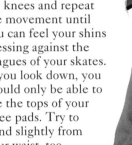

Keep looking ahead.

Stretch your arms out in front of you.

Lean from your ankles.

Your shins should touch the tongues of your skates.

4 Raise your arms and bend them slightly. Your weight should be forward on the balls of your feet, over the first and second wheels of your skates. This is the ready position. Always remember to look where you are going!

Scissor stance

You will use this stance to glide, stop, and turn. With your feet about 6 in (15 cm) apart, shuffle one skate in front of the other until the back wheel of the front skate is beside the front wheel of the back skate.

Front wheel | Back wheel

Stroke and glide

INLINE SKATING IS about movement, which you have to create. The best way to move forward is with an action called stroking and gliding. One skate strokes to the side, which pushes you forward, while the other skate glides, or coasts, along the ground. Together, these two movements create a "stride". Remember to use small strokes when you first start out.

Stroke practice

Stand in the ready position (see page 19) with your feet in a V-stance. Imagine that your feet are the hands on a clock face – your right skate points to 1 o'clock and your left skate points to 11 o'clock.

Lean forward slightly in the direction that you are moving.

Finding your balance

Being able to balance on one foot is vital to stroking and gliding, and is a necessary skill to master before you try any more advanced moves, such as crossover turns (see pages 28-29).

One-leg balance

Practice balancing on each foot by standing in the ready position and picking up one foot at a time. See how long you can stand on one leg.

Your arms should be outstretched.

Duck walk

This exercise will prepare you for your first strides. Your feet should be in a V-position, with your toes pointed outward and your wheels on their inside edges. Pick up each foot and take small steps forward.

Keep your knees bent.

Roll your ankle inward.

Inside edge

1 From the V-stance, gently push your right skate out to the side and then return it to the V. Repeat this move with the left skate to get used to the feel of your wheels rolling beneath you.

Skate style

Roll your right skate outward, keeping your left skate on the ground on the inside edges.

Glide on your right foot.

Push off with the left foot.

2 Shift your weight to your right foot as you push off, or stroke, with your left skate. Let your right skate glide forward along the ground and lift your left skate off the ground. This is your first stride!

Skate style

The stroke of the left skate propels you forward. As it lifts off the ground, the right skate glides along the surface.

Advanced striding
When you become more experienced at stroking and gliding, you can adjust your body position to give you more control over your skates. For example, note the low position and flat back adopted by the skater in this picture.

Push with your back leg.

Keep your head up.

Good posture
Remember to bend from your knees, lean from your waist and keep your head up.

Glide in the ready position between strokes.

Always look where you are going.

3 Bring your feet together and coast along on the center wheel edges of both skates while you recover your balance. You should be in the ready position, with your weight on the balls of your feet. This is called parallel rolling.

You should always be able to see your arms. This way, your weight will stay forward.

Center edges

Weight distribution
Remember to keep your knees apart and your weight over your toes.

4 Try the stroke-and-glide action again, this time pushing off with your right foot and gliding along on your left skate. Continue balancing on one foot while you push off with the other, making sure you return to parallel rolling each time. When you feel confident, try linking the strokes together.

Push your shin up against the tongue of your boot as you glide along on your left skate.

How to stop

BEFORE YOU LEARN to go any faster on your skates, it is vital that you know how to stop safely. Stopping is not difficult, but it may feel awkward at first and requires plenty of practice. There are many ways to decrease your speed and stop on inline skates, but the heel brake is the first and most efficient method you will use. Most inline skates come with a heel brake already attached. It is usually on the right skate, but can be moved to the left if you are left-handed. The brake is square or round and is usually made of rubber.

Look ahead, not down at your skates.

Keep your arms out to maintain balance.

Lean forward slightly at the waist to put more body weight and pressure on the brake.

Heel stop

The first type of braking system developed for inline skates was the heel stop, and it is probably still the most effective. Make sure you practice on grass first before moving to a flat, rolling surface.

Best foot forward
Place your brake on your strongest leg.

1 Glide forward in the ready position and scissor your feet so that your braking foot is in front. The brake should be beside the front wheel of your back skate.

2 Lift the toe of your braking skate until you can feel the brake on the ground. Don't stop suddenly – glide forward and increase the pressure on the brake gradually.

3 When the braking skate is in position, bend your back knee as you glide along. This will make you feel like you are sitting and will give you more control of the brake.

Spin stop

Like the T-stop (see page 23), the spin stop is a way of stopping without using your heel brake.

1 This sequence shows a spin to the right. From a ready position, place your right skate behind and lift up your heel. Keep the front wheel gliding along the ground.

Make sure the front wheel of this skate remains on the ground.

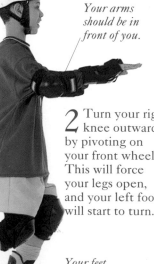

Your arms should be in front of you.

2 Turn your right knee outward by pivoting on your front wheel. This will force your legs open, and your left foot will start to turn.

Your feet should be in a scissor stance (see page 19).

Open your arms out to the side to help you balance.

3 Set your right skate down on the ground. Keep your heels together and your knees bent. Now both skates will be traveling in a spin. Keep your arms to the side and your chest up to stop you from falling forward.

Keep gliding along on this foot.

Set this skate down. Try to keep your heels about 6 in (15 cm) apart.

T-stop

1 The T-stop does not use the heel brake. Instead, as its name suggests, you stop by making your skates form the shape of a capital "T." Glide forward in the ready position. Your skates should be in a scissor stance with the braking foot behind.

Braking foot   *Scissor stance*

2 Keep your body weight centered over the front leg (here, the left leg). Slowly turn the toe of your back skate outward. You will feel the inside edges of the wheels on this skate start to drag along the ground.

Inside edge   *Front leg*

3 Keep the front skate on the center edge. Continue to drag your back foot toward the heel of your front foot to form a "T" shape. The more pressure you place on your back foot, the quicker you will stop.

Drag your wheels along the ground.   *Center or outside edges*

Wear and tear
The main disadvantage of the T-stop is that you use your inside edges to stop. This makes your wheels wear out more quickly than necessary.

Hold this arm out for balance.

Bring one arm across your chest to stop you from spinning around.

Keep both knees bent.

4 It is very important to bend both knees as you stop. Try not to turn the back skate too far to the side, or you will spin. To prevent this from happening, bring the arm that is on the same side as your back leg across your body (here, the right arm). Apply pressure from your toe to your heel on the back skate.

Slowly does it
Use this stop when you are traveling slowly, or to stop yourself from falling.

Don't forget to practice this stop to the left, too.

Keep your head and chest up to stop you from falling forward.

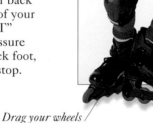

4 Your skates will automatically complete the spin, and you will stop. Make sure you finish on your inside edges with your knees bent.

Power slide

The power slide is one of the most impressive ways to stop. However, it requires a high level of skill.

1 Keep your body weight centered over the front leg (here, the left leg). Slowly lift your back skate and turn the toe outward.

2 Place your back foot on the floor in a sliding position. Make sure you angle this foot so that you slide on the inside edges of your wheels rather than your skate frame. Your upper body should be facing in the same direction as your front skate.

Falling safely

AT SOME POINT, every skater experiences the feeling of losing his or her balance or catching a wheel, and tumbling to the ground. Don't worry – falling is part of the fun of learning. The key is to land safely. The more relaxed you are, the less likely you are to injure yourself. Never try to fight a fall by grabbing at trees, fences, or even people. Instead, have faith in your protective gear and try to stay calm.

Getting up from a fall

Falling down on the ground is the easy part. However, learning how to get up properly will stop you from sliding back down into your original position. This may be entertaining for people watching but won't help you much!

Bring this leg over as you roll onto your side.

1 Begin by rolling onto your back, then your side. Start to push yourself up with your hands.

Try to lean forward when you feel yourself starting to fall.

Bend at the waist.

Don't lock your elbows.

Keep your knees bent.

How to fall

If you have ever watched a hockey game, you will have noticed that the players seldom hurt themselves when they fall. This is because they slide along the ice, which reduces the impact of the fall. The plastic on your protective gear acts somewhat like the ice, allowing you to slide along the ground.

1 Experienced skaters usually fall quickly because they are traveling so fast. However, as a beginner, you will be traveling much more slowly and can therefore often feel yourself starting to fall. Always try to fall forward if possible. Try to stay relaxed, and lower your center of gravity by bending at the waist.

Geared up
It's very important that you wear your protective gear correctly. The elastic sleeve must go around the backs of your knees and elbows. It is then tightened with the Velcro® straps.

Try to fall onto your knees first.

2 As you hit the ground, try to direct the impact of the fall onto your protective gear by landing first on your knees, then your elbows, and lastly your wrists. Keep your fingers up to avoid scraping your knuckles.

Weighty matters
If you push up from the ground with your arms, your weight will be too far forward, and you will fall over again.

Start to straighten up your body.

Slowly stand up. Keep your center of gravity low until you feel stable.

Take a deep breath to help you relax before you set off again.

Support leg

Steady yourself by placing your hands above your knee.

Try to keep your skates controlled.

2 Roll over onto your hands and knees. Keep looking down at the ground and start to shift your weight back onto your knees.

Don't lean too heavily on your hands.

3 Bring one foot under your body and place both hands above your knee. Make sure your skate is flat on the ground, then press down on your leg with your hands to stand up.

4 Bring your back leg in as you straighten up, and place both hands on your knees. Make sure you are standing correctly and feel balanced before you start again.

Regaining your balance

By lowering your center of gravity, you can avoid toppling over even if you have lost control of your skates.

Falling backward
Try to avoid falling backward – your spine is extremely delicate and can be easily damaged by the impact of a fall.

Waving your arms or legs around will not help you regain your balance.

Keep your back straight.

Bend at the waist.

1 If you start to lean backward while skating, you will overbalance. Never try to regain your balance by standing up or flailing your arms around.

2 Instead, quickly bring your arms down in front of you, bend your knees, and touch your knee pads. Glide along in this position until you feel stable enough to continue skating.

Bend your knees so that your skates are in the air.

3 Slide along on your protective gear until your body is flat on the ground. This spreads the impact of the fall through your body. If you are nervous about falling, practice each of these stages separately until you feel more confident.

Keep your head up to avoid scraping your face as you slide along the ground.

Try to keep your fingers up off the ground.

Stretch your arms out in front of you.

Turns

Keep your head up and your arms just below shoulder height.

WHETHER YOU WANT TO change direction, negotiate a corner, steer around obstacles or other skaters, or simply stop, knowing how to turn is an invaluable skill. Turns can also help you control your speed. Whenever you feel you are going too fast, link a few turns together and you will slow down automatically. The two types of turns that you should learn first are the A-frame turn and the parallel turn. Practice them in a large area with plenty of room to turn freely.

Inside edges

Keep your shoulders and hips square as you turn.

A-frame turn

1 The A-frame turn is an ideal turn to learn first because your feet are wide apart, which makes you very stable. During this turn, your body should resemble a capital "A" shape, hence the name. Try this on a flat surface or a gently sloping hill at first. Glide forward in an A-stance (see page 19), with your feet wider than your hips. Your weight should be evenly distributed over both feet. Keep your head up and your arms out in front.

Bend this knee slightly more than the other knee.

Inside skate

2 To turn left, as shown above, bend your right knee slightly more than your left. This will put more pressure on the ball of your right foot and force your right, or outside, skate, to turn. To turn right, put more pressure on the left foot.

Outside skate

Skate style
Before you attempt an A-frame turn, practice standing with your feet wider than your hips and your toes pointing straight ahead. Bend your knees and push your shins against the tongues of your skate boots. You will be on your inside edges.

Your weight should be evenly placed on both feet.

Good form
A wide stance, inside edges, bent knees, and a lean from the waist are all crucial to a good A-frame turn.

3 Keep your feet apart and your toes pointing forward during the turn. If you are on a hill, put more pressure on the outside skate.

3 Twist your upper body and your head. If you are turning left, look left. Your body will go in the direction that your eyes go. Stay in the scissored position until you finish the turn. Keep your arms out in front for balance.

Your eyes should always be looking in the direction you want to go.

Corresponding edges

You need to be on your corresponding wheel edges (see page 19) to make a parallel turn. Practice rolling onto your right skate and then your left. You should also practice leaning your body into the turn.

Steering and support skates

In a parallel turn, the front skate is the steering skate. You should put about 60% of your weight on this skate. The back skate, or support skate, should support about 40% of your weight.

Keep your head up.

Twist from your waist so that your shoulders face toward the turn.

Parallel turn

1 Glide forward with your feet in a scissored position. Most of your weight should be on your front (steering) skate. Control your speed and make sure you look where you are going.

2 Lean your body into the turn and roll onto your corresponding wheel edges. Your steering skate will be on the outside edge and your support skate on the inside edge.

Your arms should be outstretched.

Lean your entire body into the turn.

Your feet should remain in a scissored position until you have finished the turn.

Keep your knees bent.

Perfect parallels
For a good parallel turn, you need corresponding edges, a scissor stance, and a lean toward the turn.

Back, or support, skate

Front, or steering, skate

Parallel turns downhill

This skater is executing parallel turns while traveling downhill. Note the use of corresponding edges and the angle of his body as he leans into the turn. His head is up and his eyes are looking down the hill.

Crossover turns

UNLIKE A BASIC TURN, in which you simply coast along as you turn, a crossover turn allows you to maintain and even increase your speed as you turn. Crossovers are a more advanced and efficient way of turning, and they are used a lot in speed skating and inline hockey, where fast changes in direction are essential. If you are right-handed, you will find it easier to turn to the left, and vice versa. However, you should try to be proficient at crossovers to the left and right, so spend time practicing on your weaker side, too.

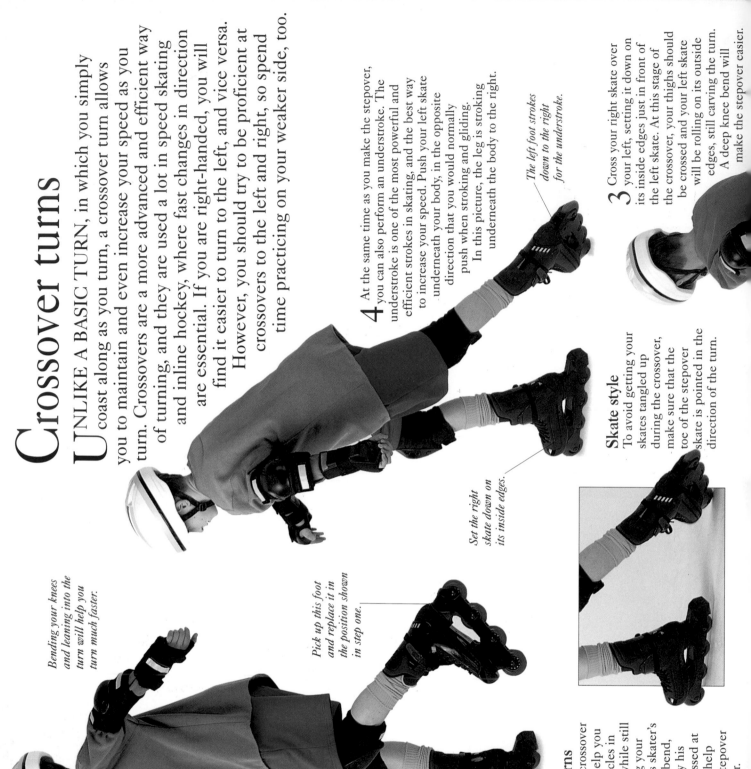

The left foot strokes down to the right for the understroke.

4 At the same time as you make the stepover, you can also perform an understroke. The understroke is one of the most powerful and efficient strokes in skating, and the best way to increase your speed. Push your left skate underneath your body, in the opposite direction that you would normally push when stroking and gliding.
In this picture, the leg is stroking underneath the body to the right.

Set the right skate down on its inside edges.

Skate style
To avoid getting your skates tangled up during the crossover, make sure that the toe of the stepover skate is pointed in the direction of the turn.

3 Cross your right skate over your left, setting it down on its inside edges just in front of the left skate. At this stage of the crossover, your thighs should be crossed and your left skate will be rolling on its outside edges, still carving the turn. A deep knee bend will make the stepover easier.

Bending your knees and leaning into the turn will help you turn much faster.

Right turn
When turning to the right, simply reverse these instructions, substituting right for left and left for right.

Pick up this foot and replace it in the position shown in step one.

5 When you have completed the stepover and understroke, put your weight on your right skate (the stepover skate) and pick up your left skate (your understroke skate). Move this skate back to the original position on its outside wheel edge, ready to repeat with another stepover.

Street turns
Mastering crossover turns will help you avoid obstacles in the street while still maintaining your speed. This skater's deep knee bend, and the way his legs are crossed at the thighs, help make the stepover much easier.

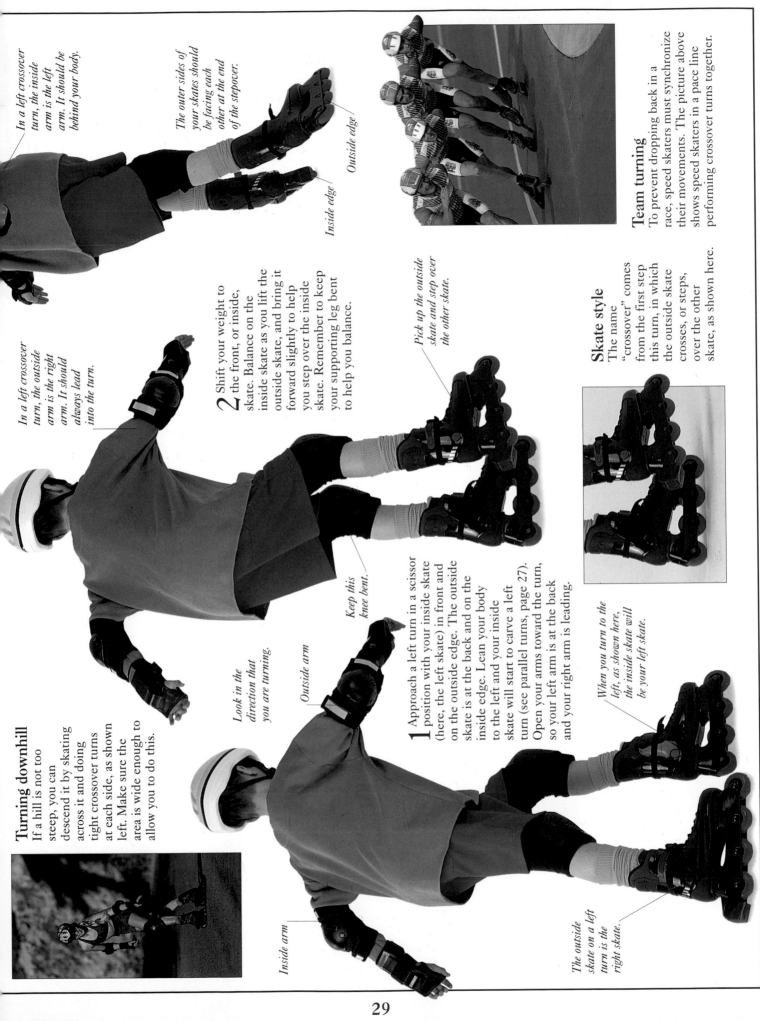

In a left crossover turn, the inside arm is the left arm. It should be behind your body.

The outer sides of your skates should be facing each other at the end of the stepover.

Outside edge

Inside edge

Team turning
To prevent dropping back in a race, speed skaters must synchronize their movements. The picture above shows speed skaters in a pace line performing crossover turns together.

Shift your weight to the front, or inside, skate. Balance on the inside skate as you lift the outside skate, and bring it forward slightly to help you step over the inside skate. Remember to keep your supporting leg bent to help you balance.

Pick up the outside skate and step over the other skate.

Skate style
The name "crossover" comes from the first step in this turn, in which the outside skate crosses, or steps, over the other skate, as shown here.

In a left crossover turn, the outside arm is the right arm. It should always lead into the turn.

Keep this knee bent.

Look in the direction that you are turning.

Outside arm

1 Approach a left turn in a scissor position with your inside skate (here, the left skate) in front and on the outside edge. The outside skate is at the back and on the inside edge. Lean your body to the left and your inside skate will start to carve a left turn (see parallel turns, page 27). Open your arms toward the turn, so your left arm is at the back and your right arm is leading.

When you turn to the left, as shown here, the inside skate will be your left skate.

Turning downhill
If a hill is not too steep, you can descend it by skating across it and doing tight crossover turns at each side, as shown left. Make sure the area is wide enough to allow you to do this.

Inside arm

The outside skate on a left turn is the right skate.

Skating backward

ONCE YOU HAVE mastered skating forward, you may want to try skating backward. At first, it may feel uncomfortable or unnatural, but as long as you remember to keep your back straight and look behind you, you will find that it gets easier with practice. All the basic rules for skating forward, such as bending your knees and ankles and keeping your weight on the balls of your feet, remain the same.

Transitions

1 To turn around on your skates, stand in a scissor position. Extend your left arm and foot forward, and your right arm and foot backward.

Scissor stance

2 With your body in the same position, lift up your heels. You will be turning in the direction shown by the blue arrow.

Backward crossovers

Before you attempt a backward crossover, you should practice sculling backward. This involves swizzling with one foot (see page 31) while the other foot glides along the ground. When you feel comfortable sculling backward on each foot, you will be ready to turn it into a backward crossover. Crossovers are used mainly for turning, so make sure you have a large area in which to practice.

Turn your head to look over the shoulder on the inside of the turn.

Your upper body should be straight and leaning into the turn.

Use your outside arm for balance.

Lead with the inside arm.

1 This sequence shows how to turn to the left. Start by using your outside skate (which in this case is the right skate) to glide backward. Your feet should be in a scissor stance (see page 19). Keep your knees bent, your left arm extended, and your weight centered over both skates. Roll your edges toward the turn.

Outside leg

Inside leg

Inside edge

Outside edge

Keep this knee bent.

Lift up this skate.

Your weight is on your inside leg.

2 Shift your weight onto your left leg. This is your inside, or support, leg. Lean your body into the turn. Keep your support knee bent and lift up your right, or outside, skate.

Keep your arms in the same position.

3 Quickly pivot on your front wheels, with your toes facing the direction of the turn (see arrow). Your arms and head should not move.

A soft landing
Practice transitions on grass first to avoid injuring yourself.

4 Your heels should now be pointing backward. Lower them to the ground. Keep your arms and head in the same position and look over your shoulder.

Swizzling backward
This is like swizzling forward (see page 35), but because you are going backward, you must look over your shoulder to see where you are going.

1 From the ready position (see page 18), point your toes inward so that your feet form an "A" shape on the ground. Twist your upper body so that you can look over your shoulder.

2 Make sure you are on your inside edges and then push both skates outward at the same time. You should start rolling backward. Keep your knees bent and your head up.

3 Center your weight over your skates and draw your feet together into a "V" shape. Practice this in-out movement until it becomes a natural, flowing sequence.

Remember to look where you are going.

Keep your arms outstretched.

Cross the right skate over the left skate.

Try to land on your inside edge.

3 Cross your right skate over your left skate and set the right skate down on its inside edge. Your legs will be crossed at the thighs. Set the right skate down so that it is parallel to the left skate.

Make sure you have regained your balance before lifting up your left skate.

Changing direction
If you want to turn to the right, simply follow this sequence, substituting left for right and right for left.

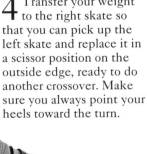

4 Transfer your weight to the right skate so that you can pick up the left skate and replace it in a scissor position on the outside edge, ready to do another crossover. Make sure you always point your heels toward the turn.

Pick up your left skate and place it in a scissor position.

Skating downhill

PART OF THE CHALLENGE of inline skating outdoors is the wide variety of hills that you will inevitably encounter. Skating down hills is exciting, but before you attempt a hill you must be able to control your speed and stop easily. Always make sure the gradient of the hill is within your skill and confidence level.

Look ahead
Always keep your eyes focused down the hill so that you can take evasive action in good time to avoid obstructions.

Traversing

The best way to go downhill is to use a skiing technique called traversing. Traversing involves a series of parallel turns (see page 27) to the right and the left. These allow you to skate across a hill instead of straight down it.

Zigzag
Traversing is the safest way to descend a hill because it helps prevent your speed from increasing too fast.

1 Keep your arms up for balance and stay in a scissor stance with your knees bent and your weight forward. You should be constantly rolling from side to side on your corresponding edges.

2 Each time you traverse from side to side, you must put your inside leg in front to lead you into the turn. Your back leg will support you throughout the turn, but you should have a little more weight on your inside leg.

Skate style
When you turn left, your left foot should be in front. At this stage, you should be on your corresponding edges.

Skate style
When you turn right, your right skate should be in front to lead into the turn.

4 As you approach the bottom of the hill, get ready to use your heel brake (see page 22).

5 If the way ahead is clear, you may want to continue skating forward.

3 If you start to go too fast, turn more so that your skates point uphill slightly. This will quickly reduce your speed.

Body position
Remember to lean forward from your ankles so that your weight stays over the balls of your feet.

Skate-to-ski
Once you've mastered traversing you can practice for the ski slopes by getting some specially designed ski poles. Parallel turns with pole planting will enable you to negotiate steeper hills. With this method of turning, there is more weight on the outside (downhill) leg.

Obstacles

HAZARDS AND OBSTACLES are another part of outdoor skating. Twigs, gravel, curbs, manhole covers, cobblestones, oil, and water can all present problems. The safest and easiest way to deal with hazards is to avoid them, but this is not always possible. Try to focus about 20 feet (6 m) ahead so that you can see obstacles clearly. This should give you time to analyze it and decide whether or not to attempt moving over it.

Your weight should be forward.

Up curbs

When you are skating outdoors, you will probably have to go up and down curbs at some point. Once you get the hang of it, hopping up curbs is simple.

Step with this skate.

1 Stepping forward onto a curb is just like walking. Glide toward the curb and shift your weight onto one skate, lifting the other skate up.

Keep your weight on this skate.

2 When your front skate is on the curb, put your weight onto it and lift the back skate up. Glide forward on the pavement on both skates, keeping your weight forward.

The side step

Approaching a curb from the side is slightly easier because you only need to take a small side step.

1 Glide toward the curb with your skates in a scissor stance. Your inside leg should be in front. Transfer your weight to your outside leg. Lift up the inside skate and place it on the curb.

Arms out

Your weight should be on this skate.

Inside leg

Balancing act
Keep your arms in front to help you balance, and look toward the curb to make sure you have stepped far enough.

2 Put your weight on the upper skate, bend your knees, and lift the bottom skate. Set it down in a scissor stance and glide forward on both skates.

Arms out for balance

Over twigs

Try to avoid hazards such as twigs, sticks, or gravel since they can get caught in your skates and make you fall. If you do skate through such things, take small steps and make sure you lift your feet up high.

Lift up your feet to stop twigs from catching in your wheels.

Down curbs

The easiest way to get off a curb is to stop and step off it; but if you want to keep up your speed, you can just skate off.

2 Simply glide off the curb. Do not jump. Keep your body in the same position and bend your knees and ankles forward to absorb the impact of landing.

Straight upper body

1 Approach the curb in a scissor stance with your heel brake at the back. Keep your weight over your second and third wheels.

Bend your knees and ankles forward.

Swizzles

Swizzling, or sculling, is another way of skating forward. It can be done slowly or at normal speed. Learning to swizzle will enable you to swerve and turn, avoid obstacles, and generally be more in control of your skates.

Bring your knee pads close together.

Keep your knees bent as you open your legs wide.

1 Stand with your heels together and your toes apart. Bend your knees and roll on to your inside edges.

2 Push your skates outward by opening your legs wide. This will get you rolling forward. Keep your weight on the balls of your feet.

3 Point your toes inward and pull your feet together again until they are back in their starting position.

Backward inverted swizzles

This is an exciting trick, which involves swizzling backward, but crossing your skates over instead of pulling them together. When your skates are crossed, you will be on both outside edges. Note that the skater is looking behind him, but his weight is forward over his toes so he can maneuver his skates more easily. You can practice this move by using small obstacles, such as cans.

Jumping

WHEN YOU HAVE PERFECTED the basic skating moves and feel confident on your skates, you may want to try more complicated skills. The jump is the main move in "extreme" skating (see pages 40-41). Extreme skating includes riding stairs, grinding rails, and jumping off launch ramps. It is thrilling to watch and to perform, but it is very difficult. Never underestimate the risk in doing some of these moves! Try to break down each of the jumps shown here into steps you can practice separately.

Dizzy heights
For experienced skaters, the thrill of jumping on higher ramps or quarter pipes is hard to beat. This picture was taken at the Street finals of the World Championships in Switzerland, and shows me catching some really big air off a high launch ramp!

Jumping with a ramp

You need lots of skill, confidence, and nerve to try this. When you first learn, it's a good idea to ask two friends to help you. They can skate on either side of you, holding onto your hands lightly and supporting you as you ride off the ramp. This will help you build up the confidence to do it on your own. Always wear full protective gear when attempting any kind of jump.

1 Mark a chalk line 10 ft (3 m) away from the ramp. Build up speed on your approach to the ramp, and then, when you reach the chalk line, start to glide.

Bring your arms up to give yourself more momentum as you push up into the air.

You may want to hold on to your boots while you are in midair.

Keep your arms in front for balance.

Start to bring your knees up to your chest.

Your body should be in a deep ready position as you approach the ramp.

2 Just before you reach the top of the ramp, try to give yourself an extra push to add more height to your jump. At this stage, you should be looking ahead, roughly at the area where you are going to land.

3 As you lift up high into the air, tuck your knees up toward your chest. This much tighter body position will give you more control. Remember to keep looking forward and concentrate on lifting your whole body over the ramp, not just your skates.

Launch ramps
Make sure you use a professional skate ramp. Never try to build one yourself – it could collapse.

Remove your heel brake before attempting any jumps to avoid getting it caught.

Learning to jump

Body position, weight distribution, and speed are the keys to jumping. When you first start jumping, it is a good idea to begin with small jumps before progressing to something bigger. Try jumps from a standing position at first, and then insert a short glide.

Bring your arms back to provide the momentum that you need to get into the air.

1 Lean forward from your waist and bend your knees deeply. Pull your arms back.

Stand with your feet in a scissor position.

2 Keeping your body straight, jump up into the air. Bring your arms forward to help you balance.

Push off from your toes as you lift up into the air.

Remember to keep your head up.

3 Bend your knees when you land. Make sure your feet are in the scissor position.

Let your knees start to drop from their tucked position.

Start to move your feet into a scissor position.

4 At the height of your jump, you will start to drop down toward the ground. Lower your knees slightly from the tucked position and start to scissor your feet.

Look at your landing point, not your skates.

6 When you land, try to bend your knees deeply to absorb the impact of hitting the ground. Keep your feet in the scissor position and your arms in front as you glide forward. Make sure you are properly balanced before you start striding forward again.

Keep your knees bent.

Your strongest leg is behind.

A heavy landing
The higher you jump, the heavier you will land, so always make sure that you bend your knees when you land to avoid injury.

5 Extend your legs and position your strongest foot at the back of the scissor position to give you better balance and support. Try landing with first your right foot behind you and then your left foot to discover which one feels the most stable and comfortable.

Taking it farther

THERE IS MUCH MORE to inline skating than simply skating around a park or rink. Once you have worked on the fundamental skills and feel really confident, you may want to use these as a basis for trying different aspects of skating. It is often a good idea to join a club that specializes in a specific type of skating because it will offer expert coaching, as well as the chance to compete against other people and make new friends. No matter which skating activity you choose, it will keep you fit, healthy, and active for years to come!

Downhill skiing

Inline skating is very similar to skiing. This makes skating ideal for ski training during the summer months, when there is no snow around. The picture above shows an inline skater practicing the "tuck" position for ski racing. You should be confident about traveling downhill quickly before you try this.

Inline hockey

The inline skates of today were developed by ice-hockey players looking for a way to play during the summer. Inline hockey players are among the most accomplished inline skaters. The game is faster and more physically demanding than ice hockey, so it is played in two 15-minute halves. When you play, you should wear protective gear, and ideally have skates that are specifically designed for inline hockey.

Speed skating

Speed skaters adopt a low position, a powerful stroke (push), and a long glide. They wear helmets and wrist guards, but other protective gear restricts movement. Speed skates have long frames and up to seven large wheels for speed. Races can be short sprints or endurance events such as the marathon (26.2 miles). Racing strategy involves tucking behind other racers to minimize wind resistance, and having a powerful sprint finish.

Inline basketball

This sport began in 1992 in New York. Each team has four players. It is a non-contact sport specializing in finesse, speed, endurance, ball-handling skills, and skating skills. Body checking is forbidden and there are limitations on jumping to minimize the risk of injury. Players wear protective gear, but not wrist guards, as it is easier to control the ball without them.

Figure skating

Inline figure-skating (or freestyle) skates use a special frame with four wheels and a rubber pik at the front. The wheels are specially rockered with the two middle wheels lying lower than the first and fourth wheels. The skater can perform spins and turns easily, while the pik enables the skater to execute jumps and aerial spins.

Land surfing

Land surfing is an exciting method of getting around on skates. It requires a large area (like a beachfront), a special sail, and windy conditions. Also, skates with larger wheels are more desirable. The sail is lightweight and easily passed over the head to change direction. It is easy to reach high speeds, so you must be confident on your skates. You will need to be able to glide in a scissor stance and execute tight parallel turns.

Cross-country skating

The first cross-country inline skates were made in 1997. The wheels are large and resemble tires with a tread. Full protective gear is very important, as is an ability to turn and jump over obstacles. These skates do not have a brake so skaters need to be proficient at alternative stopping methods.

Rollersoccer

This sport is played like regular soccer and began in 1996 in the US. It is extremely fast and exciting with quick and fluid starts, stops, and turns. It is the perfect way to learn skate skills because it gets your mind off your feet and on to the ball.

A standard soccer ball is used in rollersoccer.

Extreme skating

EXTREME OR AGGRESSIVE skating encompasses street-style and vert and is one of the fastest growing segments of inline skating. It is exciting to watch and exhilarating to do, but it carries more injury risk than other skating styles. Television coverage of extreme skating began in 1994 and was so successful that the X-Games (Extreme Games) is now recognized as the premier championship for inline skaters around the world. There are even computer games dedicated to this sport.

Born to ride
You need to feel confident and relaxed on your skates before stair riding. It is very important to maintain a scissor stance throughout, with more of your weight over the back skate. Start with one stair, then progress to two, and so on. Wider stairs are easier to master, but avoid stairs with sharp edges. Keep your speed up to prevent your skates from tripping on the stair.

When jumping, keep your weight forward and your arms in front.

Living on the edge
A curb is the best place to learn how to grind with confidence. Start by facing the curb. Jump up and lock your skates onto the curb between the second and third wheels. Hold your balance for as long as possible. Progress to jumping from a position sideways to the curb, and when you've mastered this, you are ready to try it at slow speeds.

Use your arms to help you balance.

Slalom
In slalom competitions, the aim is to skate in and out of a set of evenly spaced cones. Penalties are given for cones knocked over, but extra marks can be gained for style and technique, such as using one foot or skating backward.

Preparing to launch
Practice launching off a ramp in two stages. Using a small ramp about 24 in (60 cm) high, practice rolling up forward and backward (fakie). Next, stand at the top of the ramp and practice jumping off, landing in a scissor stance.

Fun on a fun box

The fun box in this picture has a launch ramp on one side and a landing ramp on the other. Some boxes have grind rails off to one side and maybe a set of stairs. Skaters ride up the launch ramp where they gain enough speed to perform tricks, like this front flip, and aerial spins.

Riding high

After riding the quarter pipe, you can move on to a half pipe. To get from one side to the other, "pump" by bending your knees as you turn around on the transition, then extend your legs against the pipe. Pumping will help you get higher on the ramp. When you gain enough height, try perfecting some tricks like this Sad Plant invert.

Quarter pipe

This picture shows one half of a vert ramp, also known as a quarter pipe. Find a small pipe and practice rolling up and back. Then try rolling up forward, turning around at the top and rolling back down. Gradually progress to bigger pipes, making sure you get familiar with the feeling of the transition.

Always learn to ride ramps from the bottom.

Glossary

You may be unfamiliar with many of the terms used by inline skaters. Some of the more common ones are listed below.

A
A-frame A wide stance used to start turning movements. Helps to maintain balance and a low center of gravity.
Air A jump.
Allen key A tool used to unscrew the bolts that hold the wheels and the brake in place.

The side step

B
Bearing A case containing ball bearings that are shielded and pre-packed in grease. This reduces friction and allows the wheels to spin smoothly.
Brake The rubber stop usually found on the right skate. Brakes are used to decrease speed and/or stop.

C
Center of gravity The distribution of weight that keeps you evenly balanced. It is crucial to maintain your center of gravity to avoid falling.
Coasting Forward or backward movement without propulsion. Usually involving rolling on two feet.
Coping The piping that is placed at the top of a transition. It is designed for stalling and grinding.
Corresponding edges A position in which both skates are angled in the same direction, with one skate on the outside edge and one skate on the inside edge.
Crossover An advanced turning technique used by inline skaters to turn while maintaining speed.

D
Diameter The size of the skate wheels, usually measured in millimeters.
Drop in Standing entry into a quarter or half pipe.
Duck walk A method of walking on skates for beginners, in which the feet are turned out.
Durometer A term for measuring the hardness of a skate wheel. The higher the number, the harder the wheel.

E
Elbow/knee pads Protective safety equipment with reinforced plastic and foam to protect the elbow and knee joints in a fall.

F
Fakie Rolling down a transition backward.
Flip Any move in which you rotate a full circle with your waist as the axis of rotation.
Frame The part of your skate underneath your boot which holds the wheels in place.
Freestyle General term for dancing movements.
Frontside A grind facing the curb or rail.
Fun box A many-sided platform, typically with a launch ramp up to the deck and a landing ramp on the opposite side.

G
Glide A movement similar to coasting, but with propulsion, and on one leg.
Gluteals The muscles at the back of the hip.

Finishing a transition

Grab
Grab To hold on to one or both skates during a jump.
Grind To move across a rail or curb, while traveling on a grinding area of the skates instead of using the wheels.

Inner thigh stretch

Grind plates Metal or plastic plates on the inside of skate frames to make grinding easier.
Grind rail A metal or PVC plastic pipe about 2.4 m long and 15 cm off the ground, 4 to 5 centimetres in diameter.

H
Half pipe Two quarter pipes placed together with a flat area between the transitions.
Hamstrings The muscles at the back of the thigh.
Hand plant To air out of a ramp and land supporting your body with one or both hands while keeping the legs and body extended.
Heelstop A method of stopping using the heel brake.
Helmet The most important part of your protective gear. Made with an inner shock absorption layer and an outer protective shell.

I
Inside edge The side of the wheel closest to the center line of the body.
Inside skate The skate that is closest to a turn.
Invert Performing a hand plant with one hand before reentering the ramp. Also refers to being upside down in a transition or air maneuver.

J
Japan An air where both legs are pulled back to the side while reaching around to grab the top of the bottom skate.

L
Launch ramp A small transition, usually made of wood, used to launch into the air.
Lock-on Landing both skates together on the grind plates between the second and third wheels.

M
Momentum The force with which you travel forward.
Mute A grab in which the legs are pulled up

underneath the body and one hand grabs the opposite skate.

O
Outside skate The skate that is outside or away from a turn.

P
Parallel turn An advanced method of turning using corresponding wheel edges.
Power slide A way of stopping while traveling backward.
Power strap An additional buckle to tighten the cuff or the top of a skate.
Puck A weighted disc or ball that hockey players try to put into their opponent's goal.

Pump A method of bending knees and extending legs against the pipe to gain speed.

A spin stop

Q
Quadriceps The front thigh muscles.
Quad skate The traditional roller skate.
Quarter pipe A transition that goes from horizontal to vertical and usually has a platform and coping at the top. Also half of a vert ramp.

R
Ramp A wooden or metal structure used to get air, or jump.
Ready position The stable body position that allows a skater to move in any direction.
Rockering Lowering the middle skate wheels to create a curved wheel line. Allows a skater to make quicker turns.

Rotation When inline skates are rotated to enhance their performance and make them last longer. This is especially useful when performing wheel-grinding stopping techniques such as the T-stop.

S
Sad Plant An invert where one leg is bent in and up to the body and grabbed with the opposite hand.
Scissor stance Standing in a ready position with one foot in front of the other, so that the back wheel of the front skate is beside the front wheel of the back skate.
Sit in Entering a quarter or half pipe by sitting on the edge and leaning into the transition.
Slalom Quick, sharp turns on corresponding edges.
Spacer A plastic or metal device in the center of the wheel to prevent the bearings from making contact with each other.
Spin stop A method of stopping without using the brake.
Stall To be stationary on a grinding surface or obstacle.
Stance The position of your body in relation to your balance.

Gear for night-time skating

An inline skate and different wheel types

Striding The combination of stroking and gliding in a continuous fluid motion, which can propel a skater forward or backward.
Stroke The "push" portion of a stride.
Swizzling A technique of skating in which skates are moved in and out while never leaving the ground. This creates an hour-glass path on the ground.

T
Transition The part of a pipe that goes from curved incline to flat incline.
T-stop A braking technique in which the braking skate is placed at the back of the leading leg to form a "T" shape, applying friction between the inside edges of the wheels and the ground.
Tuck A low body position adopted by inline racers.
Turning Blending skills to effect direction change and speed control.

V
Vert A term that refers to any quarter or half pipe where the transition goes from horizontal to vertical.

W
Wax Sometimes used to prepare concrete surfaces for easier, faster grinding.
Weight transfer The shifting of weight from one leg to another.
Wrist guard Protective handwear that minimizes injury to the wrists and palms. A plastic bar usually runs from the bottom of the wrist across the palm of the hand, enabling the wearer to slide along the ground.

Index

Useful addresses

These inline skating organizations and suppliers may be able to give you more information on skating clubs and coaches.

International Inline Skating Association (IISA)
105 South 7th Street,
Wilmington, NC 28401
Tel: (800) 56-SKATE
Tel: (910) 762-7004
Website: www.iisa. org
Email: director@iisa.org
Information on using appropriate safety gear and finding out where to get lessons; free booklet available.

Aggressive Skaters Association
13468 Beach Ave.
Marina Del Rey, CA 90292
Tel: (310) 823-1865
Website: www.ASAskate.com
Email: ASA@ASAskate.com

Rollerblade ®, Inc.
One Sportsystem Plaza
Bordentown NJ 08505
Tel: (800) 283 6647
Website: www.rollerblade.com

USA Hockey Inline
1775 Bob Johnson Drive
Colorado Springs, CO 80906-4090
Tel: (800) 888-INLN

USA Inline Racing
1271 Boynton St. #15
Glendale, CA 91205
Website: www.usainlineracing.com

Publications:
Inline magazine
2025 Pearl Street
Boulder, Colorado 80302
Tel: (800) 877-5281

Inline Hockey News
2025 Pearl Street
Boulder, Colorado 80302
Tel: (800) 877-5281

Kelly   Simeon   Peter   James   Barry Lee

Acknowledgments

Dorling Kindersley would like to thank the following people
for their kind help in the production of this book:

With special thanks to all the Young Inline Skaters for their skill and enthusiasm during the photography; Sarah McClurey for her technical advice at the photo shoot for pages 14/15; Sally Hamilton for picture research; Aldie Chalmers for his support and enthusiasm throughout this project; Tom Chant at Fagans, UK distributors of Bauer inline skates and Cooper hockey equipment; club blue room, London for the loan of clothes and skates for the front cover; Ray Moller and Tim Kelly for their patience during the photography; The Queen Mother Sports Centre for their hospitality.

The publisher would like to thank the following for their kind permission to reproduce their photographs:
a=above; c=center; b=below; l=left; r=right; t=top

Picture Credits

Allsport: Remy Michelin/Vandystadt 41b. **Davis Barber:** 38cl. **Sandy Chalmers/Inline Skatermag, Oxon:** 23cra, 23br. **Corbis UK Ltd:** Kevin Fleming 40bl; Patrick Ward 35r, 40br. **Tony Donaldson:** 10cl, 10br, 28br. **Mary Evans Picture Library:** 11tl, 11cl, 11c, 11bl. **Jack Gescheidt ©** **2000:** 14bl, 39tl, 39b, 41tl, 41tr.

Harmony Sports: Photo courtesy of skater Nathalie Biedermann and photographer Eric Maurer of Visiomatics (www.skatetrix.ch) 39c. **Image Bank:** 21tr, 38bl; Marc Romanelli 38tr. **Thorsten Indra:** 10tl, 10bl, 36tr, back jacket cr. **Tom LaGarde:** Heather LaGarde, 1996 NIBBL Properties. Inc 38br. **Mountain Stock Photography and Film, Inc:** Annemarie Weber 29tr; Chaco Mohler 29bl; Leighton White 0Endpapers; Nagel 33br. **Pegasus Sports International:** www.skatingaccessorie.com 39tr. **Michael Reusse:** 10cr. **Rollerblade ® Inc:** 11cr, 11br. **Stockfile:** Steven Behr 27br, 40tc, 40c.